Solomon's Cat

David Holman

**Introduction and questions by
Alison Jenkins**

HEINEMANN
EDUCATIONAL

Heinemann Educational,
a division of Heinemann Publishers (Oxford) Ltd
Halley Court, Jordan Hill, Oxford OX2 8EJ
OXFORD LONDON EDINBURGH
MADRID ATHENS BOLOGNA PARIS
MELBOURNE SYDNEY AUCKLAND SINGAPORE TOKYO
IBADAN NAIROBI HARARE GABORONE PORTSMOUTH NH (USA)

Published in the *Heinemann Plays* series 1993
93 94 95 96 97 10 9 8 7 6 5 4 3 2 1

A catalogue record for this book is available from the British Library on request.
ISBN 0 435 23297 5

Cover design by Keith Pointing
Designed by Jeffery White Creative Associates
Typeset by Taurus Graphics, Kidlington, Oxon
Printed by Clays Ltd, St Ives plc

Contents

Introduction   v

List of Characters   vi

Solomon's Cat

  Act One   1

  Act Two   37

Questions and Explorations

1 Keeping Track: Act One   55

               Act Two   57

2 Explorations: A Staging Solomon's Cat   58

               B Animal Rights   59

               C A Sense of Movement:

                 Words and Poems   60

Glossary   62

Introduction

Solomon's Cat looks at the life of an eleven-year-old African schoolboy. It's through Solomon's eyes that we witness the hardships and joys of growing up in Tanzania, where money and food are in short supply and the people have to fight for their survival, just like the wild animals that share their land. For many animals, such as the leopard, life has proved too difficult and few remain in Tanzania. That is, until one day on his way to school, Solomon sees a baby leopard and her mother ...

Ideas for follow-up work can be found at the end of the play. The first section *Keeping Track* comprises straightforward questions on the text. These can be completed orally, or in note form, as you read through the play.

Suggestions for a more detailed look at some of the issues raised in the play follow in the section called *Explorations*. Finally a glossary provides a useful reference for allusions in the text and for potentially difficult words.

Alison Jenkins

List of Characters

Solomon Mkonazi   Tanzanian schoolboy
Isaac Mkonazi   His older brother, marathon runner
Mrs Mkonazi   Solomon's mum

Julius Shaba   A schoolboy
Rosa Carvalho   A schoolgirl refugee from Mozambique
Miriam Kawawa   A schoolgirl

Miss Nyambui   Their school teacher
Ranger Filbert Mweza   National Park ranger
Rashidi Shaba   A poacher. Julius' Dad
Timothy Mwenda   A poacher
Amos Mgata   A skin dealer
Customs officer   An airport employee

Leopards, gazelles, snakes, jackals, vultures, domestic cattle, crocodiles, birds.

Possible doubling

Solomon
Rosa/Mrs Mkonazi/gazelle/Timothy
Filbert/Rashidi
Miss Nyambui/wounded cow/model/Mother Leopard
Mgata/Julius/Isaac
Miriam/Little Africa/new cow/customs officer

The action of the play takes place in and around a national wildlife park in present-day Tanzania.

Act One

Scene One

Tanzanian music is playing as the audience enters. The stage is covered with a silk cloth. In the following narration the cloth will be used to represent the sea and shore of Tanzania. The company can also use simple props and puppets such as the ship, plane delivering the food drop and the land bird as well as sound effects to accompany the narration. One of the performers does a leopard roar. Another holds up a large child's portrait of Solomon the Tanzanian schoolboy in his blue school uniform. Another holds up a child's portrait of a leopard. The following narration is shared among the cast.

Narrator Solomon and the Big Cat. Solomon is eleven years old. He is African and he lives in a country in Eastern Africa called Tanzania. A long way from us – over the sea.

So let's start our adventure and go and find Solomon in Tanzania.

Into our ship.

Away from London and South to the English Channel.

Some of the ships we pass are bringing oil from Africa.

That way's the coast of France.

And there Spain.

The Atlantic Ocean.

Into the Mediterranean and along the coast of North Africa, Morocco, Algeria and Libya.

Through the Suez Canal into the Red Sea.

We are between two worlds now. On the left Arab peoples, to our right Africans.

And getting closer now – the East Coast of Africa.

There Ethiopia. No rain. No crops. And starving children.

And there – the highlands of Kenya.

A land bird. From Tanzania. We must be close.

Yes. There are the shores of Tanzania!!

We're here!!

The Narrators sing and dance. They sing the following song: Ee vijana, vijana, vijana, vijana, etc.

Narrator   But Solomon doesn't live here on the coast. We need to go far inland.

Past coffee and cotton plantations and up over the mountains.

Over rivers where villagers are already fishing the dawn waters. And up into the highlands again as the sun rises.

This must be Solomon. They say he runs everywhere.

Solomon is seen running. He wears the blue shirt uniform of the Tanzanian schoolboy and has a school bag over his shoulder. The narrators retire.

Scene Two

Solomon   Well she won't have a chance to yell at me today, Miss Nyambui. 'Late for school again Solomon. How do you expect to help Tanzania if you can't read?' Not late. Up at six, out of the hut to milk the cattle, quick breakfast of oats and blood from the cow's neck and running! I'll be the first one there. Ee vijana, vijana, vijana, vijana, vijana, vijana tayari. Our school song. It means 'We the children of Tanzania, we are ready to help our country however we can.' Five miles to school, five miles back. Up here in the highlands – thin air. Lungs work hard. Strong. Marathon runner lungs. My big brother will be a marathon man this year at the World Games. I'm sorry. Too much talk. I'll introduce myself. Solomon Mkonazi. Abari. That's hello. Swahili language. (*He looks for a response.*) Abari. Listen,

Miss Nyambui read us a story from your country. Father Christmas. Old man. Very kind. Has wooden cart pulled by funny looking wildebeest with long horns. Gives presents to children. No charge. He never comes here. Next time you see him, ask him, for Solomon. One pair Reebok road runners. This size. OK? You ask him?

Julius speaks from off stage.

Julius   Solomon!

Solomon   My friend Julius His dad and mine work on the collective farm.

Julius speaks from off stage.

Julius   Solomon!!!

Solomon comes to a halt from his running.

Solomon   You meet Julius but don't tell him of our deal about the road runners or he'll want a pair too.

Julius has entered driving a wounded highland cow. Blood all over its side.

Solomon goes to the cow.

Solomon   Julius, what's happened?

Julius   Attacked.

Solomon   Let me see.

Julius   A lioness. From the National Park.

Solomon is inspecting the cow's side expertly.

Julius   Dad heard the cow scream.

Solomon speaks to the cow.

Solomon   It's all right. Calm.

Julius   Threw heavy iron pan.

Solomon   Not good.

Julius   Think she'll live?

Solomon   Touch and go. Deep. You taking her to Mr Bayi?

Julius nods.

I'll tell Miss Nyambui you might be late.

Julius Yes. She told me to tell you. If you're late again it's big trouble. Special visitor coming to the school today.

Solomon I'll be the first one there.

Julius speaks to cow.

Julius Hup.

Julius and the cow start to move off.

National Park animals ruin our lives. Lions attack our cattle. For what? So rich white people can come and take photos. We starve if she dies.

Julius and the cow exit.

Solomon Poor Julius. And his dad can't even spear the lion like we used to or he's in jail. School.

Solomon starts to run again. Rosa, the Mozambique girl, enters running behind Solomon. Also blue uniform and school bag over her shoulder.

Rosa Solomon, wait for me.

Solomon Rosa, today I try to break my record to school. Julius already held me up.

Rosa Oh Solomon.

Solomon Oh all right.

Solomon speaks to the audience.

This is a good example. Rosa is from Mozambique.

Bad war going on there. South Africans making trouble like everywhere. People starving. Miss Nyambui says to class 'All of you, look after this poor refugee'. So who runs especially slowly like now? And does Solomon get any thanks?

He shakes his head.

Rosa Solomon run slower.

Solomon See what I mean?

Rosa The teacher is mad at you.

Solomon What is it this time?

Rosa You. Absent again yesterday.

Solomon Had to run ten miles to Warangui. The cow was sick.

Rosa	Ten miles??
	Solomon proudly points to the horizon.
Solomon	In one hour thirty, and plenty of hills on the Warangui road.
Rosa	Your brother's name was on National radio last night. New York City Marathon, USA.
Solomon	Where did you hear a radio?
Rosa	At the village shop. I memorised the results for you. First, second and third places to Kenya.
Solomon	Africa??
Rosa	Fourth and fifth Japan.
Solomon	What about my big brother?
Rosa	Shh. Sixth place. Out of ten thousand runners. Someone who shares your blood.
Solomon	Isaac!! Sixth. Couldn't be better.
Rosa	Sixth is better than gold?
Solomon	Rosa. The World Games is in three months' time. You win gold medal now you've come good too early. Sixth. Brilliant.
Rosa	Look!
	She stops and points at the carcass of a dead animal lying on the ground.
Solomon	Gazelle.
	He stops and starts to take a look.
Rosa	Solomon, no! Snakes. School!
Solomon	Plenty of time.
Rosa	Something big killed that. Might be back.
Solomon	Catch you up.
	She runs off ahead.
Rosa	Not the Mozambique marathon girl you won't.
	Solomon approaches the carcass warily.
Solomon	Gazelle. Faster than your number one speed man, Mr Lynford Christie. 100 metres for him 10 seconds.

For gazelle five. So whatever killed this one ...
Hmm. Maybe old. No. Not old. I see this often when I
run to school. Maybe too slow to get away from a
lioness or hunting dogs. If the meat is fresh I'll turn
around and take it back to my mum. We haven't had
meat all year.

Solomon picks up a stick and pokes gingerly at the
carcass.

Snakes. Huh!!

He pokes again. There is a small pause. Another smile
from Solomon. Then suddenly a big snake whips out
of the carcass. Past Solomon and away. (This will be
manipulated by a performer. Snake could be made of
something like cotton reels attached by a wire through
their centres.) Solomon jumps in the air.

I wasn't really frightened.

There is the sound of barking from off stage.

What's this?

Solomon retreats. A jackal enters. (This is not an actor
but an actor with a pole on which the impression of
the jackal is made in a soft cloth.) Solomon whispers.

Jackal. They are always there. Like the vultures for
the scraps.

Then a vulture enters.

I'm not fighting vultures for the meat. I'll make do
with rice.

The jackal looks at the bird and barks, protecting its
food. A second vulture enters. Together the two
vultures fly at the food. (The vultures are also worked
by performers.) The jackal fights them off for a bit but
is then driven off himself. He exits ungracefully. The
vultures tear at the carcass.

When death comes to the highlands the sky will be
full of these.

Solomon is about to go when there is now a small cat-
like roar from offstage.

Little Africa speaks from off the stage.

Little Africa　Roar-r-r-r-r-r.

The vultures look around and continue to eat.

Solomon　Hmmm. I wonder what ...

A baby leopard enters played by a performer.

Little Africa　Roar-r-r-r-r-r-r.

Solomon　A baby leopard.

The vultures take to the air displeased.

I've only ever seen one in books. There used to be many here but ... Maybe its mother killed this.

The baby leopard has gambolled towards the vultures. They squawk in anger and exit.

Right. School. The mother could finish me off with one swipe of her claws.

Solomon makes a move as if to go. Then he sees that the baby leopard is heading for an until now unseen wire snare.

No! You! Cub! Not there!! Snare!!

The baby leopard gets trapped in the snare and in trying to get away pulls it tight. It howls.

Little Africa　Roar-r-r-r-r.

Solomon　Oh no!! Maybe I could ... No. Too dangerous. But it will only take me ten seconds to let her out of that snare. Problem is the mother. She smells Solomon near her cub and he's dead meat.

Solomon goes to the audience.

Listen, she's small but her claws are sharp. Can someone lend me something to protect my hand?

Solomon gets whatever he's offered from the audience.

Thanks.

He cautiously heads for the baby leopard. He is halfway there when there is an adult roar offstage.

From off the stage.

Mother Leopard Roar-r-r-r-r.

The kids may shout out to Solomon at this point. If so fine. Solomon runs back to his place.

If there has been a warning from the audience.

Solomon Thanks. That was close. Phew.

There is a pause.

But that roar didn't sound that close did it? I'm going to give it another try.

Solomon sets out to release the baby leopard. He gets to the leopard after a stealthy walk. She spits at him. He grabs for the snare and she scratches.

Little Africa Roar-r-r-r-r.

Solomon Shhh. I didn't set that snare for you, junior. Calm down. Ouchhhh. Little … Nearly there.

He releases her.

Now go and scratch your mum. Not me.

There is another big and very close roar from offstage.

Mother Leopard Roar-r-r-r-r.

Solomon sees his school bag has got twisted in the snare.

Solomon My homework!

He goes to get it. There is another closer roar.

Mother Leopard Roar-r-r-r-r.

Solomon retreats.

Mother Leopard Roar-r-r-r-r.

Solomon I'm going to be late again now.

The mother leopard enters with a roar.

Go away. My homework. Oh great. And she's right in my path to school.

The mother leopard approaches the baby leopard. The baby leopard holds up her injured paw pathetically. Expecting some sympathy. The mother gives her a clout round the head for running away. The baby leopard howls.

Little Africa   Miouw!

The mother leopard then starts licking the injured paw of the baby leopard.

Solomon   Go on. Go on. She's not badly hurt. I'm going to get into trouble again and we've got a special visitor coming.

Solomon tries to slip past the leopards. The mother leopard sees him and pounces.

Mother Leopard   Roar-r-r-r.

In doing so her paw flies into the snare. She feels it and roars and pulls away. It tightens. She utters a roar of pain.

Owwwwwwwww!

The baby leopard whimpers pathetically.

Little Africa   Miouw, miouw!

Solomon   Nothing I'm going to do about that. I'll run and tell Miss Nyambui. She'll know what to do. Run Solomon!!!

Solomon exits running. With a roar at him the angry mother now starts to drag the weighted chain off. She is followed by the crying baby leopard. They exit.

Scene Three

There is the sound of the school bell. Rosa enters running.

Rosa   Thirty-eight minutes. Nearly my record. And I beat Solomon.

Miriam enters with three trowels.

Miriam   I borrowed these for the planting. The co-op needs them back by eight.

She gives one to Rosa, still panting, as Miss Nyambui enters with a piece of paper.

Miss Nyambui   Miriam you're prefect, you take this.

She hands Miriam the paper.

The government has sent two hundred trees and

	that's where the District Council want them planted. Good. Where's Sam? Where's Juma?
Miriam	Drawing water for school, miss.
Miss Nyambui	All right. Get on with it. Your group could plant thirty before the first lesson.
Miriam	Miss, who's our special visitor today?
Miss Nyambui	Later.

Miss Nyambui smiles and exits.

Miriam checks the paper.

Miriam	Right. A deep hole here. And one here. I'll dig over here.
Rosa	What's all this for, Miriam?

Miriam starts to dig.

Miriam	The District Council says we've cut down too much firewood. Plant trees, hold the soil together.
Rosa	It's bad here. Topsoil almost gone.
Miriam	We can save it. Thirty trees. Where's Solomon? Where's Julius? Men!

Julius arrives out of breath and running.

He catches his breath hard.

Julius	Am I late? Where's Miss?
Miriam	Yes you are late Julius. I'm the prefect.

Miriam hands Julius a trowel.

Get digging.

He begins to dig.

Julius	Our cow's dead.
Miriam	How?
Julius	Lioness from the National Park. We'll starve.
Miriam	Dig.

Miriam speaks to Rosa.

We might all starve. The tractor's packed up again. Broken drive shaft. And with the maize to plant. Julius go and fetch three of those saplings.

Julius nods, gets up and makes his way out.

Julius   They've got a new tractor at Warangui village. Ford. Beautiful blue.

He exits.

Rosa shouts.

Rosa   Julius, have you done the English homework?

Julius re-enters with the saplings

Julius   No. Just the Swahili. They speak funny the English. 'How do you do?' 'Will you take a cup of tea?'

They all laugh and continue digging as Miss Nyambui re-enters.

Miss Nyambui   Well done children. Excellent. By the time you are grown up there'll be a new forest here. A little deeper holes Julius. Let's give the roots a good chance.

Julius   Yes Miss.

Rosa   Miss who is our special visitor?

Julius   Yes, who is it Miss?

Miss Nyambui   Later.

She looks around.

Julius, did you give Solomon my message?

Julius   Yes Miss.

Rosa   Miss, Solomon started out to school very early.

Miss Nyambui points sarcastically.

Miss Nyambui   And? Can't read. Can't write. The only thing he is good at is excuses. His big brother sends us money from his running but Solomon can't even run to school on time.

Solomon now enters behind Miss Nyambui. He is tip-toeing and totally silent. His finger is at his mouth as a signal to his classmates not to let him down. Miss Nyambui speaks without turning round.

Can you Solomon?

Solomon freezes, amazed. She still doesn't turn around.

Late and take your finger from your mouth.

He does so rapidly. She still does not turn around.

And no homework!

Solomon Ughh?

Miss Nyambui Let me guess. A lion ate it.

The whole class falls about laughing.

Solomon looks amazed that she has got so close.

Solomon No Miss. A leopard. Well I don't know ate. But she took it.

Miss Nyambui turns violently.

Miss Nyambui Solomon Mkonazi, everyone knows all the leopards in this region have been killed by poachers. You are a naughty lying boy.

Solomon No!!

Miss Nyambui You are always bottom of the class …

Solomon It's snared and …

Miss Nyambui I am not listening.

Miriam Nice try Solomon.

Miss Nyambui You will sit here for the whole day and you will not say a word.

Rosa tries to stand up for Solomon.

Rosa Miss.

Miss Nyambui Not one word!!!

The sound of a helicopter can be heard.

Julius Miss! Helicopter.

Miss Nyambui Wait here children.

Miss Nyambui exits.

Julius Wow. A helicopter in our village!

Miriam speaks to Solomon mocking him.

Miriam Leopard!

Solomon It's true.

Rosa I don't like helicopters.

Julius	They're great.
Rosa	My dad was killed by men from one of those.
Solomon	Rosa this one isn't military.
Julius	It's from the National Park.
Solomon	The guys who protect the wild animals from poachers.
Miriam	It's landing.
Solomon	OK Rosa?
Julius	This must be our special visitor.
Miriam	Look who's getting out!
Solomon	The big guy?
Rosa	Who is he?
Miriam	That's the famous Ranger Filbert!
Julius	He's dead. It was on the news.
Miriam	Does he look dead, Julius?
Solomon	He'll believe me.
Rosa	Why is he famous?
Miriam	You hadn't arrived. A month ago. Inside the National Airport. Here. Four ivory smugglers. Getting tusks out of the country in boxes marked ornaments.
Julius	They bribe people at the Airport.
Miriam	Julius I'm the prefect and I'm talking. Here. Ranger Filbert. On his own. He told the gang they were arrested.
Julius	Blam.
Miriam	Blam.
Julius	Blam.
Miriam	Julius!

There is a pause. Julius is silent.

Blam. Four gangster bullets. He fell.

Julius	But it gave his men time to grab them.
Miriam	Julius, I was just going to say that.

Solomon	Four bullets and he's still piloting a helicopter.
Miriam	Oh no, Miss! She's reading our essays on the National Park to him.
Julius	So that's why he's here.
Miriam	She said we should write the truth. What we thought of the Rangers.
Julius	Ohhhh.

They rush to sit down as they see Miss Nyambui approaching. She enters with the uniformed Ranger Filbert Mweza. He is bandaged at head and body. Filbert carries the essay papers.

Miss Nyambui	Children our special visitor, Ranger Filbert Mweza.
Filbert	Habari.
All	Nzuri.
Filbert	Maraheba.
Miriam	Sir, your bullet holes. Where are they?
Miss Nyambui	Miriam!
Miriam	Miss, the class want to know politely. I'm asking as a prefect.

Filbert points to his torso.

Filbert	Here three.

He then points to his leg.

Here one.

Miriam	Can we see them?
Filbert	If I have to change my bandage perhaps.

Excited at the prospect Solomon has his hand up.
Miss Nyambui speaks very firmly.

Miss Nyambui	No Solomon!
Solomon	But …
Miss Nyambui	No!!

Solomon pulls his hand down and she signals him to go to the corner. Ranger Filbert with the first of the essays tries to read it.

Filbert	Who is … J?
Miss Nyambui	Julius.

Julius puts his hand up.

Filbert	And this one?

Filbert tries to read it.

M?

Miss Nyambui	Miriam.

Miriam puts her hand up. Filbert hands them their essays.

Filbert I'm glad you children were honest. The Government wants honest criticism. We make many mistakes. Now, how many other fathers dislike the National Park as much as your fathers do?

Julius Plenty Sir.

Miriam Most Sir, that have farms along the edges of the Park.

Filbert Why?

Julius Last night one of your lions killed our only cow.

Miriam Last month elephants trampled our maize crop.

Filbert Was this reported to the village council?

Both Miriam and Julius shake their heads.

Filbert Because they don't think the Government will listen. I'm the son of a poor farmer. I know what it is to lose the little you have. I'll speak to the village council about this. Tell your fathers, give me a week to set things right. OK?

Both kids nod. They look surprised and pleased.

In your essays you told me the names of the animals Allah set down in this part of Tanzania so many years ago.

He nods at them to throw some names in his direction.

Miriam Elephants. Giraffes.

Julius Zebras.

Rosa	Snakes. Gazelles.
Julius	Hippos.
Miriam	Rhinos. Wildebeest. Hartebeest.

Julius speaks with feeling.

Julius	Lions.
Miriam	Leopards.

Filbert holds up the snares.

Filbert   And all in danger. For some it is too late.

Filbert points to the snares he is carrying with him.

In one hour in the National Park I found two hundred snares set. In one hour! These have finished the leopard in this part of Tanzania.

Solomon   Sir.

Miss Nyambui   Solomon. You dare!!

Filbert   If we are to win this war we need kids like you to be our eyes and ears. We believe National Parks are the best way to save our animals. There may be better ways, but we are sure these gangs must be stopped.

There is a sudden pain in Filbert's leg.

Ahhhhh.

Miss Nyambui   Filbert!!

Filbert clutches at his leg.

Filbert   I'm all right.

Miss Nyambui   Sit still. I'll change your bandage.

Miriam   Sir, you said we could see your bullet holes.

Miss Nyambui   Miriam!

Filbert   If I said so, I said so.

Miriam   Awwwww.

Miriam speaks to Solomon as Miss Nyambui gets the bandage.

I knew she had a new boyfriend. It's him.

Solomon whispers.

Solomon	Never. What would a hero like that see in her?

Miss Nyambui is taking the old bandage off.

Filbert	If you see these gangsters with snares you must not approach them. Run to a Ranger and tell them what you've seen.

Miriam asks about the bullet wounds now the bandage is off.

Miriam	Sir?
Filbert	Quickly then.
Julius	Aw yea.

They wait to see if they have Miss Nyambui's permission.

Miss Nyambui	Five seconds.

Julius and Miriam come to him and look, Rosa is just behind them.

Miriam	Wow! Deep.
Julius	Like a crater in Mount Kilimanjaro.
Miriam	Wow.
Julius	Sir, was it a forty-five?
Miriam	Will the hole ever disappear?
Miss Nyambui	That's enough. Back to your places.

They return to their places. Miss Nyambui starts on the new bandage.

Filbert looks at another essay.

Filbert	Now who is this one. Re. O.

Miss Nyambui tries to look.

I can do it.

He speaks to the kids.

It's my eyes. Re.O.SS.A. Re.O.SS.A. Rosa.

Rosa puts her hand up.

Filbert	Rosa thinks the Rangers are doing a good job.

Filbert hands the essay back to Rosa and rises.

Good. Last one. Nothing written. Just a name at the top. Ss.

Miss Nyambui takes it and thrusts it at Solomon. Solomon takes it, ashamed.

So thank you. And kwaheri.

All   Kweheri!!

Filbert   And tell everyone. If we can't defeat the Mgata gang then more of our animals will be paraded at fashion shows in London and New York. We didn't save the leopards but other animals we can. Kwaheri.

Ranger Filbert turns to leave.

Solomon   Sir!

Miss Nyambui   Solomon I warned you.

Solomon   You have leopards!

Filbert   What?

Miss Nyambui   The boy has been forbidden to speak. He's always late.

Filbert   Miss Nyambui, we haven't seen a leopard in this region for two years.

Miss Nyambui   But I can't allow …

Julius   Let him Miss.

Miriam   Yea.

Filbert addresses Solomon.

Filbert   You've seen leopards?

Solomon turns to Miss Nyambui.

Miss Nyambui   Who'd be teacher? Yes.

Solomon   Two. One snared.

Filbert   For how long?

Solomon   An hour.

Filbert   Where?

Solomon   We can run there in half an hour.

Filbert points to his leg.

Filbert   Can't! Helicopter.

Miriam and Julius Awwww!!!!

> *They look jealously at each other.*
>
> *Filbert turns to Miss Nyambui.*

Filbert And Solomon will promise you he'll be early for school every day for a month?

Solomon Yes.

> *Miss Nyambui nods reluctantly and she agrees.*

Sir, can Rosa come? She needs to. She's been afraid of helicopters.

Filbert Too dangerous.

Solomon She's from Mozambique!

Filbert Hurry. In!

> *Both Rosa and Solomon get in to the helicopter.*

Julius You lucky …

Miriam Awww. Can we come?

> *Solomon and Rosa are miming strapping themselves into the seats. They mime the start of the whirling blades.*

Julius and Miriam Bye.

Scene Four

Solomon Look at us Rosa.

> *He speaks to Filbert.*

That way Sir.

> *The helicopter takes off. The kids exit as if being moved away from the helicopter.*

This is scary.

Rosa I know.

> *Filbert speaks into his radio.*

Filbert Ranger Filbert to Headquarters.

> *To the kids.*

You'll be OK.

To radio.

Headquarters?

To Solomon.

Keep watch Solomon. Poacher fires.

To radio.

We have a snared leopard north-east of here. I have an anaesthetic gun with me so I'll get the kids to give me a hand. Over and out.

Solomon   Sir, what's an anaes … what you said?

Filbert   Anaesthetic. It's a special gun that won't hurt the leopard. It will just put her to sleep so we can see to her injury … if she can be saved.

Solomon   Sir, how do you read all these dials?

Filbert   Someone has to show me. When I was your age and the British ruled here they didn't want young African boys to read. We had no schools. They wanted labourers.

Rosa   Sir, you could learn.

Filbert   Too late for me. Not for Solomon.

Rosa points to the ground below.

Rosa   Fires Sir!!

Filbert   Well done Rosa. Poachers.

Filbert revs up the copter.

Let's go down and give them a scare.

They dive.

Solomon points.

Solomon   There in the trees!

Rosa   Poachers!!

Solomon   They've got tusks.

Rosa   Look Solomon. Vultures!

Solomon   Hundreds of them.

Rosa   That's where they killed the elephants.

Solomon sounds frightened.

Solomon	Sir, too low! We're going to hit the trees.
	Filbert revs up the copter.
Filbert	Let's give the Mgata gang something to think about.
	Solomon puts his hands over his eyes.
Solomon	Ohhhhhh.
Rosa	We're going to crash.
Filbert	No. No. We're safe.
Rosa	Look. Look, Solomon. Poachers. Running away.
Filbert	Don't let those men see your faces. They kill our animals and they'd kill you.
Solomon	Ranger Filbert. Those trees. That's where the leopards went.
Filbert	Going down.
	Filbert lands the helicopter.

Scene Five

Filbert	OK kids out. Keep your heads down.
	They get out keeping their heads well below the whirling blades.
	Solomon runs off.
Solomon	I'll go and see if there's any sign of them.
Filbert	Wait!!
	But Solomon has already gone. Ranger Filbert looks down at the ground.
	Solomon reappears, tearing back, frightened.
Solomon	Ahhhhhhhhhh. Leopard!
	Filbert indicates to Rosa to hide.
Filbert	Rosa!!
Solomon	She's eaten my school bag and the snare's cut right into her leg.
	Mother Leopard speaks from off the stage.
Mother Leopard	Roar-r-r-r-r.

Filbert   Stay where you are Solomon!

Another roar and the mother leopard enters followed by the baby leopard. It stands there.

Mother Leopard   Roar-r-r-r.

Filbert   Solomon I need to shoot her in the neck. Turn her to you.

Solomon sounds hesitant.

Solomon   Me? How? OK (*Pause.*) Arghhh.

Mother leopard turns and roars but then turns away. Filbert has tried to line the gun up.

Filbert   No. Again but roar longer. And louder.

Solomon   I'll get closer.

Filbert   Not too close.

Solomon   Ahhhhhhhhhh.

Mother Leopard turns to Solomon.

Mother Leopard   Roar-r-r-r.

Filbert shoots. The leopard roars again looking at Filbert. Very fierce.

Filbert   Well done Solomon.

There is a pause and the baby leopard whimpers.

Solomon   Sir, you missed I think.

There is a pause and Filbert shakes his head. They wait in silence. The mother leopard crashes to the ground.

Filbert   Solomon, stay with the cub while Rosa and I see to this one.

Filbert and Rosa rush to the mother leopard. Solomon heads for the roaring cub.

Rosa, lift her leg please.

Solomon speaks while Rose is helping Filbert.

Solomon   Little cub, we didn't snare your Ma. The Ranger's trying to help.

Rosa   It's bad isn't it?

Filbert	Hmm.

Solomon speaks to the cub whispering.

Solomon That's the man who captured four of the Mgata gang with four bullets in him. Your Mum's in good hands.

Rosa Will she live?

Filbert speaks while disinfecting the wound.

Filbert Solomon, it's lucky for the National Park you saw this leopard. She's struggled so hard to get out of this snare – it's gone deep. In a day or two it would start to poison. You've saved her.

Rosa She's going to live?

Filbert All done. Let's get clear. I gave her a light dose.

They clear to the side.

And when she wakes up she'll be mad as hell.

Solomon She's going to be OK?

Filbert She'll be right as rain in a few days. Look!

The mother leopard starts to wake. She rises drugged and stumbling. The baby leopard snuggles up.

Mother Leopard Roar-r-r-r.

Filbert Solomon, Rosa. We need names for these two.

Rosa points to the mother.

Rosa The big one. Filbert.

Filbert That's a boy's name.

Rosa Filbert.

Filbert OK. Thank you. And this little one Solomon?

Solomon pauses to think.

Solomon Africa. Little Africa.

Filbert Hmm. Back!!!

The leopard has decided to depart. It comes near them.

Mother Leopard Roar-r-r-r-r.

Little Africa roars at the group, copying her mother, but a much smaller sound.

Little Africa Roar-r-r.

The leopards exit.

Solomon Sir, your radio's calling you. The helicopter.

Filbert Yes. Little Africa it is. Thanks.

He runs off.

The kids look at each other. Mighty pleased with what they've achieved.

Solomon I wasn't scared.

Rosa I was.

Solomon No. You're from Mozambique.

Rosa Well I was.

Solomon So was I. A little bit. A tiny little bit.

Filbert comes back in a hurry.

Filbert Kids, my men are arresting poachers but some have got away. There may be shooting. You'll be safer at home. So run.

Solomon Yes sir.

Filbert puts out his hand.

Filbert On behalf of the National Park, thanks.

Filbert shakes both of their hands.

Kwheri.

Rosa and Solomon Kwheri.

Filbert leaves. Rosa watches him go, while Solomon slowly inspects the hand that has shaken hands with Ranger Filbert. He shows his hands to Rosa.

Rosa You saved Leopard Filbert and Little Africa.

Solomon We all did.

Rosa I go this way. I'll see you tomorrow Solomon.

Solomon Yea.

Rosa goes.

Scene Six

Solomon   Home

Solomon starts to run.

Yes, those poachers aren't going to see my leopards
in their fashion show. Whatever a fashion show is.
Hmm. Ranger Filbert does all these things and he
can't read. So Miss Nyambui's wrong. He's doing
plenty for Tanzania. There in the village fields, our
Ford tractor. Broken down again. Sam the old driver
kicking it. They say a new one from the USA would
cost the village our coffee crop for the year. Every
year they cost more.

*There are noises from off stage. Sound of voices.
Solomon is curious and looks a little frightened.*

Rosa.

*There is no answer. He waits as footsteps come
towards him. He runs to hide. Enter two poor
poachers. One is carrying a zebra skin and the other
two small tusks.*

He whispers.

Poachers! If they saw me in that helicopter I'm dead
meat. Oh no. One of them is Julius' dad. He'll
recognise me.

Rashidi is carrying a zebra skin.

Rashidi   This skin dealer from the city? How much will he
pay for this?

Timothy   400 shilling.

Rashidi shakes his head with disappointment.

Rashidi   For a full skin?

Timothy   Better than breaking your back picking coffee.

Rashidi   Yes but 400 won't buy me a new cow. Even a calf
costs 600.

Timothy   Shhhh.

Rashidi   What?

Timothy makes a motion for him to be quiet. They listen. The sound of footsteps. Rangers. They arm themselves and spread out.

Rashidi whispers.

That Filbert. He is a magician. Mgata's men put four bullets in him and still he chases us.

They wait. The noise gets louder.

Amos Mgata speaks from off stage.

Amos Mgata   It's all right boys. It's me.

Timothy speaks to Rashidi.

Timothy   It's Mgata. I'll do the talking.

Enter Mgata. Dressed in smart European clothes with sunglasses. Maybe silvered. Smart hat.

Amos Mgata looks around.

Amos Mgata   Damn Rangers. One day I'll … OK boys. What have you got?

He looks at the booty.

I haven't come all this way from the city for this have I?

Timothy   I've got more sir.

Rashidi   Gazelle. Zebra. Eland. At our camp. Not safe to go back now.

Amos Mgata   Save your legs. You've lost it.

Rashidi   What?

Amos Mgata   I saw rangers heading for your camp. They're picking up everything.

Timothy   What are my kids going to eat?

Amos Mgata   Shut him up or I will.

Rashidi hits Timothy. The skin dealer takes out his wad of notes.

Right.

Timothy talks about the tusks.

Timothy   They're worth 2500 like before.

Amos Mgata	These are smaller. A half grown elephant.
Timothy	I had to track it for two days, sir.
	The skin dealer hands him three bank notes.
Amos Mgata	2000
Timothy	Two …
	Amos Mgata talks about the zebra skin.
Amos Mgata	This. 300.
Rashidi	No.
	Amos Mgata hands Rashidi a bank note.
Amos Mgata	Take it or leave it. If you boys want to make real money – get me a leopard. I'll pay 15,000 shillings for a full sized skin.
Rashidi	You've had all the leopards.
Timothy	No. Not all. I saw tracks this morning. Two. One full grown.
Amos Mgata	Kill it and I'll feed your families for a year.
Timothy	Rangers!
Amos Mgata	Get that stuff hidden!
	The two poachers grab the stuff and run off in different directions. They leave their snares. The skin dealer adjusts his hair and his suit. Very cool. Then he looks down and sees the snares.
	Imbeciles! Come back. I get caught with these.
	Solomon is now terrified and has tried to slip away and now he makes a sound.
	You!
Solomon	Uhhh.
Amos Mgata	Come here!
Solomon	Sir, I was just coming from school. I didn't see anything.
Amos Mgata	Here!
Solomon	Sir, Mr Mgata, please.
Amos Mgata	You've seen what happens to an animal caught in

one of these?

Solomon gulps.

Frightened? Of Amos Mgata? Listen, compared to me the man who is behind you in the trees – don't look! He gets very upset, my bodyguard, with people who look at him. I can't control him. Don't even turn boy! Upset that man and he'll pay you a visit. You won't hear him come. Always when the moon is out. And alone. Except for his friend.

He shows the snares.

His only friend.

Solomon is now very frightened.

Mgata points to the snares.

Take them, hide them.

He hears something.

Under your shirt. And run.

Solomon quickly runs to the snares and puts them under his shirt.

Dawn tomorrow. Be there or my man from Uganda will be most unhappy.

Solomon makes a last gulp and runs.

The dealer laughs and gets out his comb as we hear the sound of the lorry coming to a halt. He combs his hair and whistles.

Enter Filbert with a gun. He looks around hoping to see some booty. He searches. Mgata opens his jacket mockingly as if asking to be searched. Filbert puts his gun away. Mgata smiles.

Hey Government man. What are you going to do when they've no more use for you? An old man who can't even sign his name. Listen. A little help to certain people now and then ...

He takes out his wallet.

No one will know.

Filbert   I'll know. I'll know. A poor country tries to share the little it has equally and always there must be parasites like you Mgata. You'll pay for the animals you've brought closer to extinction and . . .

(Filbert points to his wounds.)

. . . and this too.

Amos Mgata   Those? I was in Kenya at the time.

Filbert   Going. One day I promise you.

He exits with a last look around. Mgata watches him go and shakes his head.

Amos Mgata   Pity.

He takes out a box of matches. Lights one and lets it burn.

And I promise you Government man, we'll smoke out those leopards of yours. Tomorrow.

Scene Seven

It's night time. There is the sound of mooing and cow bells. Enter Solomon now in the traditional clothes of his tribe, with his blanket ready for bed.

Mrs Mkonazi   Solomon. What's the matter? You've eaten nothing, my son. You haven't sung to the cattle. Are you ill?

Solomon feels inside his clothes.

There is a clank as he feels the snares. He looks very guilty.

Solomon   I'm all right mum.

Solomon starts to cry.

Mrs Mkonazi   Then go to sleep. I've got enough to worry about with no rice, no nothing, for tomorrow. And remember the promise you made to that Ranger. On time to school. Every day. He trusts you.

Solomon   Yes mum.

Mrs Mkonazi   Goodnight, Solomon.

And Solomon's mum exits. The sound of mooing and

the ring of cow bells continues. Solomon starts to cry.
He takes the snares from under his cloak.

Solomon   Why did he have to trust me? If I don't take these to
Mgata at dawn his bodyguard will come and strangle
me. If I do he will use them to strangle Leopard
Filbert and Little Africa. What can I do? What?

He cries again and lies down. Solomon sleeps. The
lights go down. We hear modern brash distorted
music. Lighting effects for Solomon's dream. Spotlight
in coloured light. The skin dealer, Mgata, appears in
the spotlight. He is dressed in a white dinner jacket.

Amos Mgata Ladies and gentlemen. We are so happy to be in
London again and want to show you the prize coat
from our new African collection. The finest coat in
the world.

A model appears wearing the leopard skin coat. She
starts parading to the music. As she does so …

Before I take bids for this magnificent coat I have a
big thank you to announce for a young colleague of
mine, a young friend, without whom we would never
have got these beautiful skins out of Africa.
Applause please for the real killer of these leopards
– Solomon Mkonazi. Solomon we thank you and
applaud.

Mgata and model clap. Mgata touches the coat on the
model. They raise their arms in triumph. Sound of
cheering and clapping mix with the music to a
crescendo. Spotlight snaps off. Music stops but
clapping goes on. Distorted. Solomon wakes in terror.

Solomon   Ahhhhhhhhhhhhh.

Solomon holds his ears. The clapping stops. He takes
his hands from his ears and shakes. He hears his mum
calling.

Mrs Mkonazi Solomon. Solomon. Solomon.

We hear the sound of footsteps. Solomon hides the
snares and pretends to sleep. Solomon's mum enters.

	Solomon! Solomon! What's the matter?

Solomon   Nothing Mum. I'm all right.

Mrs Mkonazi You're wet with sweat. I've never seen you like this. Can't you tell me what's the matter?

Solomon   Mum I promise I won't shout out again. I promise.

Mrs Mkonazi is hesitant.

Mrs Mkonazi But ... I hope you sleep well Solomon.

And Solomon's mum exits looking back at him.

Solomon   I won't sleep. I'll keep myself awake till dawn or I'll have that nightmare again. Tomorrow I'm the leopard killer, the killer of leopard Filbert, the killer of Little Africa.

The lights go down slowly on Solomon, awake.

Scene Eight

There is the sound of the school bell. The lights go up on Miss Nyambui ringing her school bell. Julius runs on with his school bag and in his school uniform.

Miss Nyambui Julius. There's someone here to see you.

Julius   Who Miss?

Miss Nyambui Ranger Filbert.

Julius looks scared.

Julius   Miss, it's not to do with my dad, is it?

Miss Nyambui Yes.

Julius   Oh no.

He speaks to himself.

He's found out about the zebra my dad killed. They'll put him in prison now.

The sound of a cow bell. Ranger Filbert enters with a highland cow. Julius turns.

Awwww. For my dad?

Filbert   Yes.

Julius   Aw, can I take him home now?

Filbert   Yes. And Julius?

Julius   Yes sir.

Filbert   Tell your dad. From now on we'll have no mercy on anyone poaching in the National Park. But if he behaves himself in future we'll say nothing about the zebra.

Julius   Yes sir. Thanks. Thanks.

Julius speaks to the cow.

Come on.

He talks about Filbert.

He knows. He always knows. How?

And Julius drives the cow off.

Filbert   Where's Solomon?

Miss Nyambui shrugs, her arms spread.

He promised me. Something's happened.

Miss Nyambui   He's late. That's what's happened.

Rosa enters on the run.

Rosa   Miss! Look! Up there in the highlands. Smoke.

Filbert   Fire. Big one. It's those poachers. Our leopards!

Rosa   That's Solomon's route to school.

Ranger Filbert starts to rush off.

Miss Nyambui   Oh no. Solomon. I'm going with you. Rosa, take the class for reading.

Filbert and Miss Nyambui exit. Rosa rings the bell.

Rosa   Come on children. School! Everyone into school.

And she exits.

Scene Nine

Enter Solomon in the smoke. With snares.

Solomon   Ranger Filbert. I'm sorry. I've got to take these to Mgata or that bodyguard will kill me. I'm sorry.

He exits. Smoke comes on. Enters two poachers.

Timothy	Another fire here.
Rashidi	Here. Fresh tracks.
Timothy	Today we earn that 15,000 shillings.
Rashidi	We'll need more snares.
Timothy	There's more coming. A boy from up the mountain.
Rashidi	Stand back. I'll light this dead grass now.

He lights the grass. They stand back as it flares. It forces them back. They exit. Solomon enters with the snares.

Solomon Mr Mgata, I've brought your snares. Please tell your bodyguard I've done what you told me. Mr Mgata. Mr Mgata.

And Solomon leaves coughing. He holds a hand over his mouth. Little Africa enters roaring, terrified. She looks around for escape. She is confused, she is going round in circles. She is more terrified. Solomon enters.

Little Africa, go, run!

He points to the snares.

These are to kill you! Where's your mum?

He looks through the smoke.

There! There! There she is – looking for you! Run! Run!

Little Africa is trying to scratch Solomon in her terror. Solomon hits her to the ground with the snares to force her to higher ground. Tries to be violent to get her to move. She fights back.

Little Africa Roar-r-r-r.

Solomon That way to higher ground. Run!!!

Little Africa exits, snarling at him. Solomon is relieved and starts to move off again.

Mr Mgata, Mr Mgata.

And he exits. Enter Ranger Filbert and Miss Nyambui. They are coughing.

Miss Nyambui	Look Filbert. Your leopards.
Filbert	Heading for high ground. At least they're safe.
Miss Nyambui	Come on. Solomon's in that fire somewhere.
	They exit.
Filbert	Wait. There he is.
	Enter Solomon in smoke and collapses. Miss Nyambui and Filbert approach, sweeping the smoke away. The snares are in his hand.
Solomon	The leopards?
	Filbert grabs him and pulls him to his feet.
Filbert	Safe.
Miss Nyambui	We've seen them.
Solomon	Mgata? He didn't kill them?
Miss Nyambui	No. It's all right Solomon.
	Filbert picks up the snares.
Filbert	Mgata?
	Solomon nods. He starts to break down.
Solomon	He said … his bodyguard … these … he was going to …
	Filbert comforts him.
Filbert	You've done exactly right. I've told you not to argue with these gangsters. They're killers.
Solomon	I haven't done wrong?
Filbert	You've done right.
Miss Nyambul	Well done Solomon!
Filbert	I'm paid to take the bullets. You're not. We'll get him one day.
	There is a pause. Solomon throws himself into Filbert's arms. Filbert comforts him.
	Miss Nyambui tells me that your school holidays are starting soon.
Solomon	Yes sir.

Filbert	I've just lost the use of two good men in this fire. Burnt their hands. Be off for one month at least. Bad time for me. With two leopards to study I need some help. Problem is that person would have to be able to read and write.
Miss Nyambui	That's a pity.
Solomon	Miss Nyambui, you're always telling me if I worked hard in a little while I could learn.
Miss Nyambui	It's only three weeks to the end of term, Solomon.
Solomon	Sir, don't give that job to anyone. Give me three weeks.
Filbert	Ohh … I don't know. How could anyone learn so fast? What do you think Miss Nyambui?
Miss Nyambui	I don't know.

There is a pause as Solomon looks from one to the other.

Filbert.

She beckons him. He comes over. She whispers in his ear. He nods. He nods again. We see him shake his head strongly. Then he comes ruefully across to Solomon.

Filbert	A writing test last day of term. For both of us. Yes, Miss Nyambui insists it is time for me too. Deal?

They shake hands.

Solomon	Awwwwww.
Filbert	Oh and Solomon close your eyes.

He does so.

Closed?

Solomon	Yes.

Filbert takes out a pair of Reebok Road Runner shoes.

Filbert	I was going to give you a little gift. Keep them closed. For saving our leopards. But now you've earned this. Count to ten Solomon and then open your eyes.

He places them on the ground and takes Miss Nyambui by the hand and they leave.

Solomon I can feel something by my feet. One. Two. Three. Four. What has he put there? Eight. Nine. Ten.

And he looks down and sees the shoes. He almost faints.

Road runners!! As worn by the great marathon runners from the mountains, Yifter and Dinsamo and Shahanga and my brother, Isaac Mkonazi.

He puts them on.

Now Solomon run to your pencil and you use it till your fingers bleed from writing. For two weeks you don't sleep. You write.

Music and Solomon runs off.

Act Two

Scene One

Tanzanian music plays as the kids come back in. Lights come up on Solomon, dressed in traditional costume, leaning on a staff, pencil and book in hand. He is wearing his road runners.

Solomon checks his writing.

Solomon   Dear Isaac, surprised big brother? Yes, this hand is mine. Hoping this reaches you before you fly to the World Games. Bring home a medal Isaac! Bad news first. The coffee crop isn't enough to buy a new drive shaft for the Ford. The whole village is very worried. The good news. You'll never guess what I am doing in the school holidays.

Mother Leopard speaks from off stage.

Mother Leopard   Roar-r-r-r.

Solomon whispers.

Solomon   Excuse me Isaac. I finish this later. I've got to get back to my job.

Solomon moves to a safe position as Leopard Filbert and Little Africa enter. Solomon watches as they come in and lie down to rest. Solomon whispers to audience.

It had taken some days to find our leopards but then Ranger Filbert spotted them near the river. Little Africa who had already been in danger from fire and from man, faced danger here too. At the river.

Two blue cloths are brought out by performers. (Ranger and Rosa.) They are stretched between them to make a river. They are held at about a metre from the floor. Leopard Filbert and Little Africa are asleep. Then Little Africa wakes and yawns. She goes over to the river. She places her paw in the water to play in it.

Like us. Very curious.

Little Africa puts her face in the water while her mother snores. Ominous music plays. A crocodile appears some way from Little Africa and glides towards her under the blue cloth. The crocodile model is worked by a performer. The design should concentrate on the jaws rather than the body of the crocodile. Little Africa again puts her paw in the water. The crocodile strikes. It misses, but only just. Little Africa leaps back and howls. Leopard Filbert wakes. Immediately throws herself towards the crocodile, spitting and snarling. The crocodile roars and threshes. Little Africa howls. The crocodile retreats. Mother clouts Little Africa for straying. Little Africa howls again. A performer removes the river. Mother curls up to sleep. Little Africa joins her.

Day after day of those school holidays I watched. Then. One day …

The leopards are still sleeping. A gazelle enters (played by a performer). Music. It starts to feed warily. Constantly looking around. Solomon whispers.

Gazelle. Faster than Lynford Christie. Faster than anything.

The leopards quietly wake and stretch. Mother Leopard sees the gazelle and pokes Little Africa. Little Africa gets up and gambols towards the gazelle. The gazelle turns sharply away and Little Africa falls over. The gazelle turns but finds herself heading for mother. Mother Leopard grabs its throat and twists. Mother Leopard waits for Little Africa to feed. Baby leopard goes to eat noisily. The mother leopard watches. When Little Africa is full they leave.

If the mother could not teach Little Africa to kill before the dry season came she would have only one future – starvation. Day after day I watched and no kill. Then, at last, this morning –

He hears Ranger Filbert approaching.

Ranger Filbert and Miss Nyambui! I can't wait to tell him what Little Africa has done.

He refers to his notebook.

My report is finished, but I like to sign it. Won't take a second.

He writes in the notebook.

End of report, signed Solomon. There.

He puts the notebook in his pocket.

Enter Ranger Filbert and Miss Nyambui. Ranger Filbert has his hand on Miss Nyambui's shoulder. Solomon is puzzled. He sees they are getting closer.

Uhhhh?

Filbert   Solomon.

Solomon   Sir, Miss, she's growing so fast, Little Africa.

Filbert   I want a full report.

Miss Nyambui   Yes Solomon, tell us.

Filbert   We can do better than that, can't we Solomon.

Solomon takes out his notebook.

Solomon   Yes Sir.

Miss Nyambui's mouth falls open as she sees page after page of notes.

Miss Nyambui   Written?

Filbert   It's the way we do things in the Rangers, isn't it Solomon?

Solomon   Joined up letters.

Miss Nyambui   May I see?

Solomon hands her the book. She flicks through several pages and reads.

Thursday night, Warangui village. Man tells me he has seen our leopards. Friday, 0805 hours I spy Little Africa and round her mouth – blood.

Filbert is delighted.

Filbert   No!

Miss Nyambui   At 1100 hours I find remains small gazelle. The first kill of Little Africa. She won't starve now. Solomon!

She shakes her head amazed at his progress.

Filbert Solomon now gives us reports every day.

Miss Nyambui You did it.

Filbert No. Solomon did it. And I have to keep up with him now.

Miss Nyambui takes Solomon's notebook and points to last sentence.

Miss Nyambui I got to there.

Filbert shrugs.

Filbert E.N.D. End. O.F. Of. R.E.P.O.R.T. Report. End of report.

Miss Nyambui Excellent.

Solomon Yes, sir.

Filbert S.I.G.N.E.D. Sig–ned. There's no such word. What is this? British. Why didn't they teach me to read?

Miss Nyambui Signed.

Filbert I'll never do it.

Miss Nyambui You'll do it. Last word.

Filbert S.O.L. I know this one. Solomon. Signed Solomon.

They both clap.

Miss Nyambui It's wonderful.

She gives Filbert a kiss on the cheek. Solomon's jaw drops.

Solomon addresses the audience.

Solomon Now I know why he's OK about me watching the leopards on my own or with Rosa. I still can't believe it.

He speaks to Filbert.

Sir, next week?

Miss Nyambui Solomon, it's school next week.

Solomon But sir, don't you need my help tracking?

Filbert Solomon, I'll tell what this country needs. Not ignorant guys like me, but kids at thirteen with a full education. Swahili, English, history and all of that.

Solomon   Awwww. I can read.

Filbert   Hey, do you know what an exam to get into the Rangers looks like?

Solomon   No.

Filbert   It's not like in my time. We have to take exams now. Miss Nyambui could get you through those exams.

Solomon   Me? A ranger?

Filbert   So, school!

Solomon nods.

Filbert kneels on the ground and beckons Solomon.

Solomon, touch the grass.

Solomon   Dry.

Filbert   In two weeks there will be no more grass left for our great herds of wildebeest and zebra.

Indicating with a stick in the earth.

This is us. Dry. No rain for weeks now. Away away over here many miles – and very soon – the rain will come. And somehow our herds will know. It is too far to see or smell but they will know. Hundreds of thousands of animals moving towards the rains. It is the greatest sight on earth.

Solomon   But our leopards …

Filbert   The leopards' prey is also heading for the far off rain.

Solomon   So they go too?

Filbert   Quickly into the Range Rover. We'll go and get Rosa and you'll see for yourself.

Scene Two

The Range Rover enters in a blackout with lights on. This is a toy car approximately 10 inches long with working headlights. We hear the voices of the occupants as the Range Rover travels up the hill.

Filbert	Headquarters, we're ten miles south of Warangui. I'm going to show Miss Nyambui and the kids the great treasure of Tanzania.
Rosa	But sir, where is this treasure?
Filbert	Rosa, wait till we get to the top of this hill.
Solomon	Still can't see anything Ranger Filbert.
Filbert	Not that way, Solomon. There!
Miss Nyambui	Oh look, Solomon! Rosa!
Rosa	Oh miss, a baby wildebeest.
Solomon	And there's her mum, her mum. They're heading for the water.
Rosa	Look Solomon, zebra.
Solomon	Loads of them, and the baby's joined the family.
Rosa	Sir, will they soon be moving?
Filbert	While this water lasts they will stay. And kids, watch carefully everything you see.
Solomon	Sir?
Filbert	Because in your life time what you will see today may all be gone.
Both	No!
Filbert	If we don't stop taking land from these animals, if we can't live beside them instead of destroying them, then you and Rosa may be the last generation to see these sights. It will all be history. Now let's go to the helicopter. The only place to see our treasure now is from the sky.
Rosa	Sir, are they frightened? Are our leopards there?
Filbert	Our leopards will be there somewhere, but no, Rosa, they're not frightened. They have smelt the rain.
	The Range Rover moves off and we see a model helicopter. We hear the voices within the helicopter.
Solomon	Oh Boy!!
	Look, Rosa, look! Hundreds of them, heading for the rain.

Filbert	Now Solomon, do you see why I call this the greatest sight on earth?
Solomon	I do, sir.
Rosa	There's thousands.
Solomon	Hundreds of thousands.
Rosa	Thousands of hundreds of thousands.
	Ranger Filbert, can you slow down? I want to count them.
	Filbert laughs.
Filbert	Rosa, look up ahead. You might as well try to count the stars in the sky. Don't count. Just watch.
Rosa	Wow!
Filbert	OK Rosa? Now you'll have something to tell them at school. Let's go. You think you'll remember this?
Rosa	Yes sir, yes sir. For ever.
Solomon	Oh boy!
	They exit, Miss Nyambui and Filbert arm in arm.

Scene Three

The lights go up on Solomon as he enters singing.

Solomon	Ee vijana, vijana, vijana, vijana. Big day. First day of new term and last day of the World Games. Marathon day. Go Isaac. A medal for the village.
	He runs on.
	Miriam enters behind him with radio.
Miriam	Solomon!
Solomon	Miriam! Now can I listen to my big brother's race?
	Miriam refers to the radio.
Miriam	Borrowed. My uncle. Don't tell him.
Solomon	How much to hire from you?
Miriam	How long is this marathon? Batteries are expensive.
Solomon	For my big brother, close to world best. Two hours 07.

Miriam	For anyone else ten shillings. For you five.
	Solomon hands money to Miriam.
Solomon	Deal.
	Miriam hands radio to Solomon.
Miriam	No argument about the price?
	Solomon starts to run.
Solomon	No.
	Miriam starts to run.
Miriam	Are you ill? You always argue.
	Solomon smiles and points.
Solomon	Twenty miles that way my leopards are following the wildebeest on their long long journey to the rains. And you'll never guess Miriam. A miracle. You'll never guess.
Miriam	Stop grinning like a monkey. What?
Solomon	Soon my two leopards are going to be three or four or five.
Miriam	No! Babies!
Solomon	Yes, so there's a male leopard among the wildebeest herds now. The leopards are coming back to this region.
Miriam	Which one is having babies?
Solomon	Little Africa. Wait till I tell them at school. A mum!!!
Miriam	Solomon you lucky thing. I'm the prefect. I should get these jobs.
	Solomon stops running.
Solomon	Oh.
Miriam	What?
Solomon	Didn't Miss Nyambui tell you, Miriam?
Miriam	What?
Solomon	About the change of prefect this term.
Miriam	What??????
	There is a pause. She realises.

Solomon!!!

Solomon has already started to move.

Solomon Only joking.

Miriam Come back. I get you for that. Come back.

And she chases the laughing Solomon off.

Scene Four

A single poacher enters. His eyes search the savannah. Looks up and sees his quarry. Lines up the sight and fires.

Mother Leopard Roar-r-r-r-r-r-r-r-r-r.

Timothy She won't get far now.

He exits. Enter the mother leopard mortally wounded. Groaning in agony. Little Africa enters. Moans and licks the mother. Noises off as the poacher approaches. Little Africa hears them and leaves. The mother leopard collapses – shaking. The poacher enters. The mother leopard looks at him from the ground.

Mother Leopard is defiant in her pain.

Mother Leopard Roar-r-r-r-r-r-r.

The poacher pulls the trigger. Leopard Filbert dies. The poacher gets out his knife.

Timothy 15,000 shillings.

Then he looks down at the tracks of Little Africa.

And tomorrow another 15,000.

Fade to blackout as poacher starts to skin the leopard.

Scene Five

Two squawking chickens enter. These are manipulated by a performer. Solomon enters carrying radio and bowl of chicken feed.

Radio Radio Tanzania. This is Radio Tanzania reporting

live from the World Games. Join us in five minutes for the start of the marathon where our very own Isaac Mkonazi is in sparkling form.

Solomon is satisfied and turns off the radio. He starts attending to the squawking chickens.

Solomon   Shoo. Shoo. Eat that and lay some eggs for the school farm. We've got a production target for you two and you're not keeping to it. Rosa!!! So lay. I've only volunteered for this until my leopards come back from the migration. You're no match for my leopards, you two.

Rosa enters behind him.

I haven't got time to waste. Rosa and me have got maize to plant while we listen to the marathon.

(*Sings.*) Ee Vijana, vijana, Vijana, tayeri (*twice*)
          Kulitumikia, Taifa, Taifa, Taifa.
          Kultitumikia, Taifa, Taifa, Tanzania.

Miss Nyambui enters smiling.

Miss Nyambui   You two sound happy!

Solomon   You too miss.

Rosa   Miss what's …

Miss Nyambui hands Rosa a paper.

Miss Nyambui   Bless your big brother, Solomon.

Rosa reads.

Rosa   Ford Motor Company. USA.

Miss Nyambui   He has saved the village.

Solomon   Isaac? But he hasn't won his marathon yet.

Rosa continues to read.

Rosa   We deliver to you one tractor drive shaft. Paid in full.

Solomon   His sixth place dollars from New York!!!!

Rosa   Drive shaft?

Solomon   It's the big metal, Rosa. From wheel to back axle. Expensive. Isaac!

Miss Nyambui is about to exit.

Miss Nyambui	Expensive and heavy to lift. The village men are at Warangui. I'll walk there, get four of them and their lorry.
Solomon	Can we come?
Miss Nyambui	Finish here and I'll pick you up when we take the drive shaft to the tractor. In three or four hours.
Both	Hurray!!
Solomon	Miss, did a customs officer from the National Airport bring the drive shaft?
Miss Nyambui	No, it came by road.
Solomon	Well then, what's she … Rosa, there again!
	They see the Customs Officer.
Miss Nyambui	She's a long way from the airport.
Rosa	That's what we thought.
Miss Nyambui	Mmmmmm. Kwaheri.
Both	Kwaheri.
	Miss Nyambui exits.
Solomon	Drive shaft!!
Rosa	Maize.
	Solomon goes to the radio.
Solomon	Marathon.
	He turns up the radio as Rosa gets down to plant.
Radio	Radio Tanzania speaking. On the starting line the race favourites, the Kenyans and the Ethiopians who have dominated marathon running this year. Can anyone beat them?
Solomon	Yes, Isaac can!! Tanzania!!
Rosa	Solomon, is that planting maize?
Solomon	It's the way my Dad does it.
Rosa	No. Miss showed us.
Solomon	There. That woman from the National Airport again.
Rosa	Dig a hole every six inches. Plant. Then water.
Solomon	That'll take us all night!!

Rosa   What you were doing wastes seed. We can't afford it.

Solomon starts to dig.

Solomon   All right. Turn on the radio. I'm digging.

Rosa turns on the radio.

Radio   They stream out of the stadium this mass of world class distance men, led by the African, and at the front, with twenty-six miles to go our very own Isaac Mkonazi.

Solomon rushes to the radio in a panic and turns it off.

Solomon hides.

Solomon   Rosa. Hide!

Rosa   Why?

Solomon   Over here! The radio!!

Rosa grabs the radio and then hides by Solomon.
Amos Mgata enters with a box marked 'ornaments'.

There's Mgata. The gangster!

Rosa   Is that him?

Solomon is now totally hidden.

Solomon   If he sees me I'm dead meat. He won't have forgotten those snares. Is there a giant bodyguard with him?

The woman from the National Airport enters.

Rosa   Just that woman in uniform walking this way towards him.

Solomon   Get down!!!

Amos Mgata   And tell your customs friends, careful with this one, it cost me 15,000 shillings.

Solomon   Oh no. Those poachers have killed Leopard Filbert.

Amos Mgata   And I've been promised another of these tonight.

Airport Woman   Six boxes for the London flight.

She shows him a paper.

That's my price.

Amos Mgata gets out his wallet with bad grace.

Amos Mgata   Thieves. You take the skin from my back. You people.

She takes the money.

Airport Woman Let's go.

Amos Mgata and Airport woman exit.

Solomon They've killed Leopard Filbert. I know they have. And now they're going after Little Africa.

Rosa You've got to warn Ranger Filbert.

Solomon How? He's at the migration. It's twenty-five miles west.

Rosa Then Miss Nyambui.

Solomon She won't be back for three or four hours.

There is a pause.

Twenty-five miles.

Rosa Solomon.

Solomon Rosa. Run to Warangui. Try to catch Miss Nyambui up. I'm running for Ranger Filbert.

Rosa But …

Solomon My brother ran a marathon when he was thirteen.

Rosa You're eleven. And in this heat?

Solomon points to the radio.

Solomon Take this. Too much weight.

He turns to go.

Rosa Good luck Solomon.

Solomon And to you. My brother did it. I can do it.

Rosa then runs off.

Solomon starts to run. Slowly lights fade almost to blackout.

Scene Six

The lights come up again. We are a long way into Solomon's run. His form is much more ragged. He is exhausted.

Solomon Must save Little Africa. Must save Little Africa.

Twelve miles. So hot. Further than I've ever run. I'll never do it. I've got to do it. My brother will be on the finishing stretch of his big marathon run now. Nineteen or twenty miles now. He sent the village a postcard of the World Games city. Buildings as tall as Mount Kilimanjaro. Said he felt good. I don't, Isaac. I haven't got much more strength and there's still thirteen miles to go. I'll never do it. I'll never do it.

Music changes and slowly approaching from behind Solomon comes the spirit of Isaac Mkunazi, at this moment running the World Games Marathon.

Isaac Mkonazi   Little brother!!

Solomon   Isaac?

Isaac Mkonazi   A marathon man doesn't let his head rock little brother.

Solomon   But you are at the World Games.

Isaac Mkonazi   Six miles to the stadium and the tape.

Solomon   Where are you placed Isaac?

Isaac Mkonazi   Leading group little brother.

Solomon   Who's with you?

Isaac Mkonazi   The Australian and two Kenyans here.

Solomon   Yes.

Isaac Mkonazi   And here an Ethiopian, a British, and my friend Saleh from Djibouti.

Solomon   Africans doing well, Isaac.

Isaac Mkonazi   How do you feel on your first great journey to the twenty-six mile tape?

Solomon   Can I tell you the truth? I'm not going to make it. I'll never run another thirteen miles and Little Africa will die.

Isaac Mkonazi   What do you see out there on the savannah? Half a mile ahead? Then a mile ahead.

Solomon   Half a mile? There's a tree. And another half mile – elephants. A large herd.

Isaac Mkonazi   Forget the thirteen miles. That's too much. Think of the tree. That's your race. It's a half mile run. You make the tree, you've won your race. Then another half mile race. You will make for the elephants.

Solomon I'll try, Isaac.

Isaac Mkonazi The Kenyans are making a push. They can see the lights of the stadium. I will have to match them. Hear the crowd in the stadium little brother?

The sound of 100,000 people can be heard in the distance.

Solomon I hear them. Go for gold Isaac. You think I can do it big brother?

Isaac Mkonazi You're a highlander. Think of the tree. Don't think how tired you are. Think of your Little Africa.

And Isaac Mkonazi disappears. The sound of the crowd fades to silence. Solomon runs on.

Solomon The tree. The tree. The tree.

There is a pause. He runs on.

I'm reaching the tree. I'm reaching the tree. I've done it. Up ahead the elephants. Still there. I can do it. It's only half a mile. I'm coming Little Africa. Now for the elephants. The elephants. The elephants. Little Africa I'm coming. I'm coming to do it. Don't be killed. Little Africa. I'm coming.

Solomon continues to run.

Scene Seven

Enter Ranger Filbert with field glasses and radio. He gets down on his knees to feel an old poacher fire.

Filbert speaks into his radio.

Filbert Ranger Filbert to Headquarters. I've searched all day and no signs of poachers here. I think our leopards are safe, so I'm coming in. Over and out.

Filbert sees something in the distance.

Dust. Something running. It looks like … It can't

be ... He's at the school farm. He's fallen over. It is a boy. It's Solomon.

He grabs his radio.

Filbert to Headquarters. Contact Miss Nyambui. Something must have happened at the village. Find out what. Out. Twenty-five miles at his age. In this heat. It's impossible.

Solomon enters totally exhausted. He sways. He falls into the waiting Filbert's arms.

Solomon   Sir! Little Africa

And he keels over.

Filbert   Solomon!!

Filbert gets his water bottle and holds it to Solomon's lips.

Drink, Solomon. It's all right. Take your time. What about Little Africa?

Solomon   Mother. Killed. Poachers. Today. Little Africa.

Filbert lifts Solomon.

Filbert   Just relax. You've done a Ranger's job. Just relax. You're going to be all right. Come on.

Filbert takes Solomon off in his arms or over his shoulder. The poacher Timothy enters. He is searching the ground for tracks. He finds one. He exits following it. Solomon and Ranger Filbert enter. Filbert with gun. He searches the ground.

Poacher. Fresh. And Little Africa. Are you OK Solomon?

Solomon still swaying with exhaustion.

Solomon   Yes.

Filbert   We've got to find them before the poachers do. According to your report she's going to have her babies any day.

Solomon   She could be having them right now.

Filbert   Hurry.

They exit following the tracks. Little Africa enters very slowly and painfully. She lies on the ground. She is preparing to give birth. There are sounds from off stage – the poacher. The poacher enters.
Little Africa exhausted tries to roar. The poacher stalks her. Little Africa looks at the poacher. Poacher raises his gun and shoots. Little Africa dies.

Timothy Another 15,000 shillings. I won't starve this year.

He moves to skin the leopard. Solomon enters and sees dead Little Africa.

Solomon Noooooooooooooo.

Solomon runs to the body. Filbert has entered. As the poacher sees Filbert he drops the gun and skinning knife.

Filbert speaks to the poacher.

Filbert The last leopard in the region and you slaughter her for a few shillings. If I wasn't wearing this uniform you know what I'd do to you.

He aims the gun at him.

You'll join your boss in jail.

Filbert shakes his head and turns away.

The last one. After all this.

Filbert is cast down. There is a pause. Then the sound of a tiny meowing. Filbert looks round to where Solomon is crouching over the skinned leopard. Solomon is reaching under the animal.

Solomon! Solomon! Solomon!

Solomon Can they live? Away from their mother?

Filbert They'll live if I have to take over the National Hospital. We'll save them.

Filbert takes one.

We'll save Little Solomon.

Solomon And Little Tanzania.

Filbert speaks to the poacher.

Filbert You. Into the helicopter. Do anything that I don't like and I'll chuck you out at two hundred feet.

The poacher goes. Filbert takes off his Ranger bush hat with badge.

Solomon, of the Rangers.

He places the hat on Solomon's head.

How's that going to sound?

Solomon looks at him.

Solomon   It's going to sound good isn't it.

Filbert   Wear that while you are looking after our leopards, Junior Ranger Solomon.

Solomon   Hear that Solomon? Hear that Tanzania? I'll take your mum's place until you're big enough to come out here to the savannah and run free. Oh boy. OH BOY.

Fade to blackout and music rises.

Questions and Explorations

1 Keeping Track

These questions are here to make you stop and think carefully about what's happening in the play.

Act One: Scene One

1 As the audience enters Tanzanian music is played. See if you can get hold of some to listen to. (Triple Earth Records – telephone 071 3885533 – sells records of Tanzanian music.) How does it compare with the music you usually listen to?

2 Look at a map of the world and trace the steps of the journey through France and Spain, North Africa to Tanzania on the east coast of Africa.

Act One: Scene Two

1 Julius, Solomon's friend, complains:

'National Park animals ruin our lives. Lions attack our cattle. For what? So rich white people can come and take photos. We starve if she dies.'

What is Julius talking about here? Is tourism always a good thing for a country?

2 Solomon cannot believe it when he sees the baby leopard. He says:

'I've only ever seen one in books. There used to be many here but ...'

What do you think has happened to them and why?

3 Solomon wants to release Little Africa from the snare. At this point he actually goes to the audience to ask for something to protect his hand. '*Can someone lend me something to protect my hand?*' This is quite an unusual device for a playwright to use. Why do you think that the writer wants the actors to be so friendly towards the audience?

What do you think of this idea?

Act One: Scene Three

1 At Solomon's school, it is part of the curriculum to plant trees. This is quite different from the lessons of British pupils. Why is this?

Earlier we read that their school song is about helping their country however they can. Try to think about all the ways in which the children help their country as you read through the rest of the play.

2 Miss Nyambui is angry with Solomon for not bringing his homework. When she says: '*Let me guess. A lion ate it.*' what sort of tone of voice is she using?

Of course, she is very close to the truth, but does not believe Solomon's excuse, calling him a ' ... *naughty, lying boy*'.

Think of a time when you have told the truth, but have not been believed. How did this feel?

3 The children tell Ranger Filbert that the wild animals are interfering with their farms. Find the part in the play where they say:

'*Last night one of your lions killed our only cow. Last month elephants trampled our maize crop.'*

Which animals do you think it is more important to protect, the wild animals, or those belonging to the villagers?

Act One: Scene Six.

1   Solomon comes across two poachers. Read up to where Amos Mgata arrives. From what Julius' dad, Rashidi, says, we can begin to understand why he is poaching, even if we do not approve. What are the reasons he gives?

Act One: Scene Seven

1   Solomon is in a terrible dilemma. His life is threatened, yet he wants to save the leopards. What should he do?

Act Two: Scene One

1   Take a close look at part of this scene with Little Africa and the crocodile. Plan carefully how you would put this onto the stage.

    What type of costumes would you use? Would you make use of puppets or masks? How would you build up the tension as the crocodile narrowly misses Little Africa?

2   When Ranger Filbert finds it difficult to read he says:

    'What is this? British. Why didn't they teach me to read?'

    He has complained about this much earlier in the play (try to find that passage too).

    Why didn't the British want the Africans to learn to read? Is this fair?

Act Two: Scene Five

1   We hear some of the radio commentary of Isaac Mkonazi's
    marathon race. In what ways does a radio commentary
    differ from one on the TV?

    Plan and record your own radio commentary of an
    imaginary race, perhaps a 100m or 200m sprint. Ensure
    that you speak really clearly so that the people listening
    have a good idea of the race.

2   The customs officer is very far from the airport. Can you
    guess why she's there?

Act Two: Scene Six

1   In order to save the leopard, Solomon decides to run to
    Ranger Filbert at the migration. It's twenty-five miles away.
    Why is this number particularly important? How many
    miles is a marathon?

2 Explorations

A Staging *Solomon's Cat*

Plays are really written to be watched by an audience. Think
about how you would put *Solomon's Cat* onto the stage.

Both Leopard Filbert and Little Africa are written to be played
by actors. The actors will have to think carefully and work
hard to use their bodies and voices effectively. What advice
would you give to someone who is attempting to represent a
leopard? Think about the ways the animals move, and the
noises they make.

Where could the actors go in order to watch and learn from real leopards?

Other animals in the play are to be represented by puppets. Have a go at making these puppets from any junk that you can get hold of. (By using junk, you will be doing precisely what many African children do to make their own toys.) Some very unlikely junk will make really effective puppets. Here's just one idea to get you started:

Think about how you would make the vultures … . Why not use an old black umbrella? The tatty edges of the umbrella could represent the vulture's wings, and by putting the umbrella up and down, you could easily create the sinister sound and motion of the bird in flight.

Try to come up with ideas for all the animals in the play. (You'll find a list of them at the beginning to remind you.)

Good luck!

B Animal Rights

Many of the issues dealt with in the play are not that straight-forward; sometimes, in fact, they are rather confusing. One example of this is the issue of how people should treat animals.

The Fur Trade

Many animals are trapped and killed each year simply for their fur (LYNX put the figure at 100 million). This results in many animals being in danger of being wiped out. Some, like the seamink, have already become extinct. It tends to be the animals with the most beautiful fur that are the main targets; tigers, jaguars, mink, and of course, leopards.

Furs with bullet holes in them are worth less money so other, often more cruel ways are found to kill the animals. They may be smashed over the head, suffocated, electrocuted … .

All this happens even though seven out of ten people think it's wrong to kill animals for their fur.

What do you think about killing animals for their fur?

Try to think of any reasons: Why we should do it?
Why we should not do it?

Do a survey to find out whether people in your school think it's fair. Show the results on a graph. Now create a poster showing your opinion. Plan it carefully, you are trying to communicate exactly how you feel.

Some useful tips: Think about the layout.
What sort of picture or image will you use?

Make a quick drawing of how you imagine Rashidi to look. Think about how he feels as he has to make these difficult decisions. Put his different thoughts into speech bubbles. An alternative idea would be to write a page from Rashidi's secret poaching diary.

C A sense of movement: words and poems

Solomon's Cat is a very active, lively play. People and animals are constantly on the move; whether they're escaping, migrating, running in the World Games, or running to save Little Africa.

This idea of movement is reflected in the language. Try reading the following extract aloud:

'Must save Little Africa. Must save Little Africa. Twelve miles. So hot. Further than I've ever run. I'll never do it. I've got to do it … I'll never do it. I'll never do it.'

As you read this aloud, what effect do the short, jerky phrases have?

How do they make you sound?

Can you find any other parts in the play, written in a similar 'breathless' way?

Now try to write your own 'movement' piece along the same lines.

Choose from: The Race
Late Again!

Before starting you may wish to try to get hold of copies of the following poems, which will help you with ideas.

Night Mail by W H Auden
Breathless by Wilfred Noyce
Tarantella by Hillaire Belloc

Glossary

Page

1 *Tanzania*   country on the east coast of Africa

10 *maize*   corn

14 *habari*   hello

14 *Nzuri*   and to you too

14 *Maraheba*   thank you (you are most kind)

18 *Kweheri*   goodbye

28 *Uganda*   country to the north of Tanzania, in Africa

46 *Ee vijana, vijana, vijana, tayari Kulitumikia, Taifa, Taifa, Taifa Kulitumikia, Taifa, Taifa, Tanzania.*   We, the children of Tanzania are ready to help our country however we can.

50 *Djibouti*   country on the east coast of Africa at the mouth of the Red Sea

50 *savannah*   grassy plain